Simple North Indian Vegetarian Recipes

By Vijay Luxmi Sudera

Contents

1. Vegetable soup

Ingredients:

Potato	2 medium
Carrot	2 medium
Onion	1 medium
Tomatoes	2 medium
Spinach	Few leaves
Salt	according to taste
Pepper	according to taste
Mixed herbs	1 to 2 pinch
Soy sauce	4 table spoon

Method:

1. Wash all the vegetables and boil them until they are soft.

2. Mash them and add a little bit of warm water liquefy.

3. To the soup, put one spoon of butter, salt, pepper, soy sauce and mixed herbs.

4. Boil to preferred consistency.

5. Best served with toasted bread or bread sticks.

2. Vegetable curry

Ingredients:

Potato	1 medium
Carrot	1 medium
Rai (mustard seeds)	1/2 teaspoon
Sunflower or olive oil	1 tablespoon
Salt	according to taste
Turmeric	1/2 teaspoon
Tomato puree	1 tablespoon
Green chilli	1-2 chillies

Method:

1. Wash all the vegetables, then slice or dice them to preferred size.

2. Put oil, rai, turmeric, puree and salt in a pan then mix under medium heat. Stir for about 3 minutes, until the paste is a deep red in colour.

3. Add ¼ cup of water and add all the chopped vegetable. Cover it to steam cook on medium heat. Stir regularly to prevent vegetables sticking to the pan. Add a green chilli or two depending on taste.

4. Stop cooking when vegetables attain preferred softness. This curry is best served with chapatti.

3. Mashed Aubergine (Bharta)

Ingredients:

Large Aubergine

1 Onion and ½ a cup of peas

Oil	2 tablespoons
Salt	According to taste
Garlic paste	1 tablespoon
Garlic cloves	2-3 cloves
Tomato puree	1 tablespoon

Method:

1. Wash the aubergine and grill it until the outer skin is burnt, turning sides to allow even cooking.

2. Once grilled, peel and discard the burnt skin leaving the aubergine flesh. Chop the aubergine flesh with a knife into thin slices.

3. Slice the onions into long thin slices. Then, put oil, onion slices, garlic puree and salt in a pan. Mix and heat until onions are golden brown in colour.

4. Add the tomato puree and stir for 5 minutes.

5. Add the aubergine flesh into the pan and mix it well under medium heat.

6. Stir regularly for 15 minutes until brown in colour.

7. Bharta is best served with chapatti.

4. Cauliflower and peas (Gobi mutter)

Ingredients:

Small cauliflower	Cut into small pieces (3 cm)
Peas	¼ cup
Olive/sunflower oil	3 tablespoon
Salt	According to taste
Fresh ginger	Grated 1 tablespoon
Turmeric	1 tablespoon
Tomato puree	1 tablespoon
Fresh Coriander for garnish	

Method:

1. Cut the cauliflower into small buds of about 3cms in length and wash them.

2. Add oil and ginger in a pan under low heat. Stir to slightly cook the ginger.

3. Add turmeric and salt to the pan and keep stirring it to prevent the ginger from sticking to the pan. Stir for a minute.

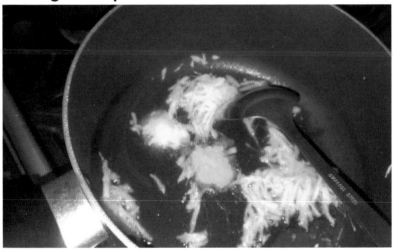

4. Add tomato puree and ¼ cup of water and then cook until most of the water has evaporated from the mixture (masala).

5. Add cauliflower to the masala sauce and stir well for 3 to 4 minutes

6. Cover and place the pan on medium heat (steam cooking is done by the water released from the cauliflower). Stir regularly to prevent the cauliflower from sticking to pan. It usually takes 15 minutes to steam cook, but can be left longer depending on taste i.e. if one prefers a hard or soft texture to the cauliflower.

7. After uncovering slowly stir the mixture to get an even spread of masala and it is ready to be served with chapatti.

5. Chilli Paneer

Ingredients:

Paneer	One block- 200 grams.
1 green pepper	
Oil	2 tablespoons.
Salt	½ spoon or according to taste.
Soy sauce (preferably dark)	6 tablespoons
2 Onions	
Garlic paste	2 tablespoons.
Tomato puree	2 tablespoons.
2-3 Green chillies	
Cherry tomatoes	handful
Iceberg lettuce	2-3 leaves

Method:

1. Cut the block of paneer into 1 cm cubes.

2. Fry them for 2 to 3 minutes in a deep pan or a wok, until they become golden brown in colour.

3. Dry the paneer on a paper towel to remove excess oil.

4. In a separate pan add the diced onions and garlic puree. Fry them in 2 tablespoons of oil on medium heat for 3 minutes.

5. Add 1/3rd cup of water (50 ml) to soften the mixture. Then add the pre-cut green pepper and green chillies. Stir the mixture to cook evenly and to prevent the mixture from sticking to the bottom of the pan.

6. Add 2 tablespoons of tomato puree and cook under medium heat to remove the excess water. Cook until the onions achieve slight caramel colour.

7. Add the cubes of paneer to the masala. Cover mixture for a few minutes to steam cook the chilli paneer.

8. Add a handful of cherry tomatoes and cook for 2 to 3 more minutes.

9. **Add five to six tablespoons of soy sauce to give a dark colour to the mixture and serve the paneer on a plate covered with strips of cut lettuce leaves.**

6. Chilli Pizza

Ingredients:

Mild/mature grated cheddar cheese	70g
Soy sauce	1 teaspoon preferably dark
Garlic paste	½ tablespoons.
Tomato puree	1 tablespoons.
Green chilli	1 cut into small circular pieces.
Tortilla	1 round 10 inch tortilla

Method:

1. Add the tomato puree, garlic paste, cut up chillies and soy sauce in small bowl and mix.

2. Slightly wet the tortilla on both sides and place it on some aluminium foil on a grill pan. Place the grill pan under the grill set too high for 1 and a half minutes.

3. Remove the tortilla from the grill and slightly butter the top of the tortilla.

4. Turn the tortilla with the buttered side down and place a tablespoonful of the paste in the middle of the tortilla.

5. With the back of the spoon, cover the whole of tortilla with the paste evenly. Other herbs or olives can be added depending on taste.

6. Spread the grated cheese evenly on the tortilla and place it under the grill set to high.

7. **After 2 minutes remove the chilli pizza from the grill and it is ready to be served.**

7. Crispy Potato, Onion and Spinach Pakora

Ingredients:

Chick pea flour	150 grams.
Potato	1 medium sized.
Onion	2 medium sized.
Spinach	100g of young leaves.
Garlic puree	1 tablespoons.
Turmeric	½ teaspoon.
Green chilli	1 cut into small circular pieces.
Garlic	2 to 3 cloves
Salt	1 teaspoon
Ajwain (Carmon seeds)	½ teaspoon
Garam masala	½ teaspoon
Olive/sunflower oil	1 to 2 litres

Method:

1. Peal the potato and dice it into 1cm squares. This prevents them being left raw. Cut the onion into long moderately sized slices. Wash the spinach and drain excess water. Then chop the spinach to a reasonable size (1 cm wide)

2. Place the chopped potatoes, sliced onions and spinach into a large mixing bowl.

3. Add ½ a teaspoon of salt depending on taste, ½ a teaspoon of turmeric, ½ a teaspoon of ajwain, 3 to 4 chopped garlic cloves, 1 tablespoon of garlic paste, ½ spoon of garam masala and chopped green chillies.

4. Add the 150 grams of chick pea flour to the mixture and mix it well so that the potatoes, onions and spinach are covered with the flour.

5. Pour the oil into a wok for deep frying (4 cm depth). Put the wok on low heat so that it is heats up while the mixture continues to be prepared.

6. Add to this mixture roughly 100ml of water and mix well. Take a tablespoon of the mixture and turn it upside down. If the mixture is thick enough to stick to the spoon when overturned, it is ready to be fried. If the mixture drops off easily then add some more chick pea flour to achieve the required thickness. Often the consistency does depend on the amount of water in the potatoes, onions and spinach.

7. To check if the oil is hot enough, place a pea size amount of batter into the wok. If it fizzles, the oil is ready. The batter should not be left standing for long as the water from the potatoes and onions will start to thin the mixture and it will require more chick pea flour.

8. Take a tablespoon full of the batter, holding it just above the oil. Using another spoon carefully slide the batter into the oil.

9. Repeat this until the wok is ¾ full. Turn the heat to medium.

10. After 3 to 4 minutes the sizzling reduces and it is time to turn the pakoras over using a skimmer.

11. Then, after 2 minutes just turn them around regularly using the skimmer to achieve even cooking. Once the pokaras have achieved a golden brown colour, drain them with the skimmer.

12. Place them on a paper towel to remove excess oil. The pakoras are ready to serve with any sauce you prefer.

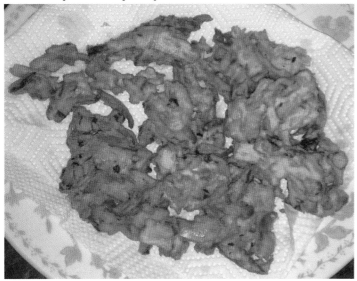

8.   Notes

Printed in Great Britain
by Amazon